AUTHENTIC LIVING

SUCCESS. MIRACLES AND SPIRITUAL LAWS

Dr. Brenda Hattingh

Authentic living. Success, miracles, and spiritual laws

Copyright © 202020 by Dr. Brenda Hattingh.

All rights reserved. No part of this book may be reproduced
or transmitted in any form or by any means,
electronic or mechanical, including photocopying, recording,
or by any information storage and retrieval system,
without permission in writing from the copyright owner.

Disclaimer.
Any use of the suggestions, skills and tools covered in this book,
and other books are used at the readers own discression.

ISBN: 9798557524209

Editing by David Barraclough from Copy-Writing
email: david.barraclough@copy-writing.co.za
Graphics by Gerhard Snyman
Website: http://www.gerart.co.za;
email: info@gerart.co.za

Published by Currency Communications (Pty.Ltd)
Johannesburg. RSA

For additional copies or e-books see:
www.amazon.com/books/brendahattingh

AUTHENTIC LIVING

SUCCESS. MIRACLES AND SPIRITUAL LAWS

Dr. Brenda Hattingh

Currency Communications Int.
Johannesburg.

CONTENT

Contents
BACKGROUND 6
INTRODUCTION 11
THANK YOU 15
ABOUT THIS BOOK 16
   The era of authenticity 19
   Success and miracles 20
   The Real-me-revolution 20
   Ultimate success 21
   What are miracles? 22
      ☐ Miracles - causing you to smile 23
      ☐ A course in miracles 23
      ☐ Miracle are thoughts manifested 23
   Who can create miracles? 24
      ☐ Prayer and meditation 24
      ☐ Universal blessings 24
   Creating miracles in our lives 25
   The spiritual laws of success and creating miracles 25
      ☐ The One Law 26
      ☐ Miracles - a natural way of everyday living 26
   Summary of spiritual laws 27
      ☐ The Law of Oneness (the Law of Unity/Universe) 27
      ☐ The Law of Right use of Power or energy/life force ... 28

- ☐ The Law of Effortless Ease (Flow and Freedom) 29
- ☐ The Law of Detachment..29
- ☐ The Law of Non-Judgement..30
- ☐ The Law of Resonance (Attracting or repelling forces) 32
- ☐ The Law of Abundance...33
- ☐ The Law of Intention (Deliberate Creation) 34
- ☐ The Law of Paradox and Polarity.................................36

Law, principles, and guidelines..36
- ☐ A law 36
- ☐ Principles..37
- ☐ Guidelines 37

QUESTIONS 38
EXERCISES 39
WHO IS THE AUTHOR - DR BRENDA HATTINGH?..............42
ENROLL FOR A PERSONAL 5-WEEK COACHING COURSE. 43
BOOK DR BRENDA HATTINGH AS SPEAKER 45
BOOK DR BRENDA FOR LEADERSHIP TRAINING..............45
MORE BOOKS IN THIS SERIES...46
CURING CORRUPTION..47
AUTHENTIC LEADERS IN ACTION 48
REFERENCES 49

OoooOooo

BACKGROUND

A motorcar accident came as a major shock and without any warning, I found myself in intensive care with fractured neck vertebrae. I couldn't walk.

Everything that I had known to be my life up and till then, had suddenly fallen away. I was in dire straits.

I knew that nothing would ever be the same again.

Burn-out

The most shocking part was, that after several weeks, my body had not started to heal. I instinctively knew that the journey back to recovery would be long and arduous.

The decision to make peace with my situation was a turnaround point. I decided to turn a seemingly bad situation into an adventure that is, adding value to every venture = adventure.

I became still – and went within.

The question I asked was: Why is it taking me so long to heal and get back on my feet?

The answer was: I was totally burnt-out. My energy reserves were depleted.

I had overextended who I was. My fuel gauge was showing empty and danger signals were going off.

The next question was, why? The answer was because I was so busy doing, helping, planning, teaching, lecturing, taking care, and looking after others, I neglected to take care of myself.

The next question followed. Who is this self I needed to take of? I always thought that we had to deny the self and be of service to others.

I didn't have an answer to this question. My belief system had shown me a different path. I was taught that it was selfish to think of self. I thought life was all about self-sacrifice. I didn't *really* know who I was.

The journey in search of self, my authentic self, had begun. During this time, I also needed to learn how to heal myself.

Finding the authentic self

I found that we have two sides of self. On the one side, we find our authentic self that is connected centered, and grounded in universal power, wisdom, and love. This part of self lives according to universal laws, purpose, and direction. It is born out of love, governed by wisdom, and has the authority and power of the Divine Universe.

On the other side, we have a shadow ego-self.

The ego-self, formed from the teachings, messages, influence, opinions, feedback, and input from others and the world around us.

These two parts of the self are directly in opposition to each other. You can only live one, or the other.

I named my shadow ego-self Elaine. What Elaine had achieved, wasn't too shabby. The price, however, was very high. She had depleted all our life force and was on the brink of dying a slow and painful death.

I knew this had to stop.

The journey back to self

My journey back to health and healing included recovering and developing my authentic self, Brenda. I had to learn to master myself while overcoming the control of my shadow egos-elf, Elaine, in my life.

The time in bed now became an adventure.

My question was: What does a healthy, balanced, whole successful, happy, fully functional, human-being look like?

I realised what I needed was a blueprint of who I am, as an authentic person. Secondly, I needed a map showing the way to a healthy, wealthy, happy, fulfilled, balanced, quality life.

To me, this sounded like a tall order.

Going back before we go forward.

I went back to my academic and religious background, in search of answers. With a B.Sc. degree in medical science, a Master's degree in Education, and a Ph.D. in Psychology,

I tapped into already available information. It left me confused. So, I decided to go to our religions.

This placed me on a new path. Many of our ancient religions still hold the keys to healing and manifestation.

This valuable information is only obtainable by word-of-mouth. You also had to go through initiations to be trusted with these wisdoms. I joined a group of fellow travelers and specialists in this field and visited Peru, Egypt, and Turkey.

Here I found people being able to master the elements, heal the sick, and manifest out of Source. This took me back to Cameron's films on this subject that included stories like the *Last Airbender.*

To most people, this is all fiction. To others, with more knowledge, wisdom, and deeper understanding, this is real.

For the first time, I started to see the light at the end of the tunnel.

Seeing the light

The days, weeks, and months in bed became a haven. Here, in the silence, solitude, and simplicity of a bedridden situation, I could discover who I really am and what the purpose of my life is. I knew that then, and only then, could I be of real service to others.

At the same time, the Human Genome Project started releasing their findings. It became clear that we had a DNA blueprint that contained all the necessary information for us to lead a life of health, wealth, happiness, and prosperity. We just needed to get connected and tap into this power and potential, once again. To do this we needed a new understanding, skills, and tools.

Three books emerged during this time.

- New Success DNA. What is it and how to develop it
- Power Intelligence. Mastering your miracle mind
- New Leadership DNA. Developing enlightened leaders.

These three books contain all the basic academic, medical, scientific, and spiritual information you will need when embarking on this journey of authentic self-discovery. The series of book and courses in *Authentic Living and Leading* emerged from this background research

It took me more than a year to heal and walk again. By that time, the books were completed, and I was ready. It was time to get back to this reality.

The accident and time in bed became a blessing in disguise.

It has taken me 17 years to research and develop all this information. I knew when the time was right, people would be asking for this and it would be ready. It is now packaged in the series *Authentic Living and Leading*.

INTRODUCTION

The era of authenticity is here. Not only does this signify a whole new mindset, but it also includes a paradigm shift and a quantum leap. A quantum leap is a leap into a whole new dimension. Some will be able to make this leap. Others will stay behind.

To make this leap, we need to start at the beginning. It is time to go back to our roots. However, our original roots are not found in our family, culture, religion, or country. It goes much deeper than that.

As said, over the last 17 years, I have spent all my time and energy researching the topics related to authentic living and leading.

Three major books cover the science, academics, psychology, and spirituality behind recovering our DNA-blueprint. This includes New success DNA, Power Intelligence. Mastering your miracle mind, and New Leadership DNA. Developing enlightened leaders.

In the series *Authentic Living and Leading,* we will take it step-for-step in recovering our authentic self, encoded as our original DNA-blueprint.

The series includes a series of books and courses that each cover a specific topic of authentic living and leading.

As summary, you find the book: *Authentic living. Recovering your Success -DNA*

Books in the series that are already available are:

- My Authentic self. Who am I?
- Coaching yourself to ultimate success
- Authentic leadership. Recovering your DNA leadership-blueprint
- Authentic Living. Going for gold – Mining your success-DNA.

An authentic life is a life that takes a stand against corruption. Corruption is the opposite of authenticity. Two books are available:

- Curing Corruption. What YOU can do to solve the real pandemic of our time
- Curing Corruption. 7 things you can do to solve the epidemic of our time

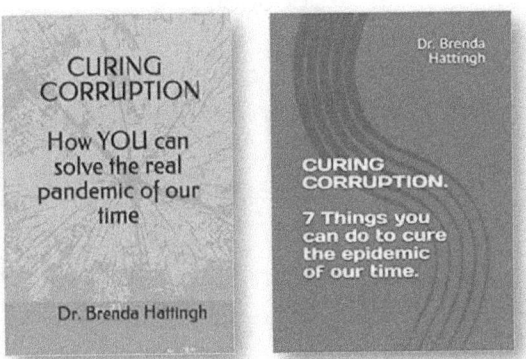

The following books in the *Authentic Living and Leading* series will be launched by Jan 2021.

- Power Intelligence. The intelligence of the future
- DNA. Climbing the new ladder of success
- The era of authenticity. Will you make the leap?
- Success, miracles, and spiritual laws

Each book covers a specific topic although they overlap. Repetition of new concepts has a positive spin-off as the information creates a whole new mindset.

Books are available on Brenda Hattingh amazon author page: Amazon's Brenda Hattingh Page

Make sure you are on our mailing list to receive information on upcoming courses and special events.

Enjoy the adventure.

oooOooo

THANK YOU

It is not possible to do all this work alone. I therefore need to thank all those who supported me during this time of self-discovery that tuned into a research and development project.

My deepest love and gratitude go to my children who have supported me and my work over the years, in so many ways.

To Gerhardt Snyman, a refined and gifted artist, my deepest thanks for the graphics and to David Barraclough and Mark Mattson who edited all the work. My deepest appreciation for your fine focus, insight, and attention to detail.

You all walked the extra mile and I know you will all be equally blessed.

My deepest gratitude goes to all my teachers, mentors, guiding forces, and masters, who invested in me, my life, and my personal success process.

I am forever humbled by the constant teaching, guidance, and unconditional love I receive.

At the same time, I am grateful for the knowing and understanding that life is part of a divine appointment, and it inspires me to continue…

From my heart—to your hearts…

Brenda Hattingh.

ABOUT THIS BOOK

This book is book nr. 5 in the series of *Authentic Living and Leading.*

The era of authenticity is here. Humanity is not only undergoing a mind-shift, but a whole quantum leap is taking place. In the process, people are recovering their DNA success-blueprint. New, authentic leaders are emerging. These are our new pathfinders and mapmakers leading us into a whole new future. Part of this new future is the ability to create miracles.

As the shift takes place, new laws become evident. Up and till now, humanity has mainly been living by their own laws, the law of the shadow ego-self. Now a shift is taking place in who the lawmaker is. People will now begin to live the next season of success and happiness, by adhering to spiritual laws. These are the laws of authenticity, truth, honesty, and integrity. These are the laws of the authentic self.

In this book, you will find answers to the questions

- What is authentic living?
- What is authentic success?

- Why does 'success' differ from person to person?
- What is a miracle?
- What are the spiritual laws that govern a quality life and miracles?
- How can I create a life of health, wealth, happiness, and quality living?
- Can I become a miracle maker? How?
- Some people will stay behind. Others will make the leap.
- Where do you stand?

You are invited to join this adventure and join hands with like-minded people.

OooO0ooo

For more information see the book. Power Intelligence. Mastering your miracle mind, chapter 18

oooOooo

SUCCESS, MIRACLES, AND SPIRITUAL LAWS

> *"Can you be still and look inside? If so, then you will see that the Truth is always available, always responsive"*
>
> Lao Tzu

The era of authenticity

The era of authenticity is here. With it comes a whole new mindset and heart-set. This is not only a paradigm shift but also includes a quantum leap. This is a leap in consciousness. People are waking up.

Higher laws are coming into play as people become mindful and aware. We are shifting from the shadow ego-self as the lawmaker, to the authentic self who adheres to higher, universal, spiritual laws. These laws apply to everyone. These are the laws of health, wealth, happiness, success and prosperity.

We are accessing a whole new level of honesty, truth, integrity, and authenticity. On this higher level, we find health, wealth, happiness, success, and prosperity. Here we can create a whole new reality. We can even learn to create miracles.

We are embarking on a new journey. We are miracles in the making.

Some people will be able to make this leap. Others will unfortunately stay behind. If you are ready – then this journey is for you. It is time to take the leap.

Success and miracles

Miracles have been part of the human experience since the beginning of time. It is well known that miracles were performed in ancient and biblical times.

There were many people like Jesus, who could change water into wine, manifest bread out of the ether, and heal the sick. The disciples of Jesus Christ were taught to perform miracles while healing the sick, as part of their service to humanity.

So do we have the right and the privilege, to learn to be ultimately successful, and that is how to create miracles.

Our real challenge is to learn how to create our 5-Star life with effortless ease.

The Real-me-revolution

In previous books in the series *Authentic Living and Leading*[1], we found that we have a DNA success-blue in every cell of our body.

This DNA-blueprint contains all the necessary information for us to create a life of health, wealth, happiness, and success. We also learn that we have two sides of self. On the one side, we find the authentic self, the real-me, or higher self. On the other side, we find the shadow ego-self.

Unfortunately, humanity lost its authenticity when we became disconnected and started functioning on lower levels of fear, anxiety, struggle, discord, and disintegration. The shadow ego-self has ruled the lives of individuals, groups, cultures, countries, and humanity for millennia.

Now an awakening is taking place. A Real-me-revolution is taking place in the silent chambers of the souls of people who hear the call to move to the next level. The Ream-me-evolution is gaining momentum as people want out of the old system – while recovering who they are and living the life they were created for. People are asking for something new, something with substance, something authentic, real, with meaning and purpose.

Success is now taking on a whole new dimension.

However, success means different things to the real-me authentic self and the shadow ego-self. While the authentic self is in search of truth and authenticity, that includes creatin miracles – the shadow egos-elf is just interested in quick fixes, immediate gratification, and acquiring power positions and blingy possessions.

The Real-me-revolution is going to change all of this.

Ultimate success

True success is about developing the ability to live our authentic self and all it stands for. Part of this success=strategy is to learn how to create a quality life with effortless ease and perform miracles for the benefit of all.

Authentic living and leading mean developing self-mastery, learning these skills, and teaching others to do the same.

This is what the *Authentic Living and Leading* series is all about.

The questions then are:

- What are miracles?
- How do we create miracles?
- Who can create miracles?
- Why haven't religious leaders taught their followers how to create miracles until now?
- What role do spiritual laws play in creating miracles?

The answer is two-fold: Very few people know much about miracles, although this is an essential part of all religions.

Secondly, the miracle-consciousness has always been available but is only starting to surface and gain entry into mainstream thinking and believing - now.

It's time.

What are miracles?

Miracles are events that appear to be unexplained by the natural laws of nature. For example, a sum of money arrives out of nowhere, just when you need it; someone calls while you were thinking of them, your deepest desires and needs are met, seemingly by coincidence. You need to relocate to a new city because of a new job offer and your home sells within three days.

These things happen 'out of the blue', and are viewed as being supernatural in origin, or 'an act of God'.

- **Miracles - causing you to smile**

The original word 'miracle' comes from *mirus*, meaning 'causing one to smile'. At the same time, it refers to 'mirror', or an occurrence that mirrors something/someone else.

For our definition, we can say: *Miracles are wonders occurring out-of-the-blue that make us smile*[379]. Miracles confirm, 'so above— so below'. Miracles are God smiling down on us, and then we smile too and smile back.

- **A course in miracles**

The book, *A course in miracles* says that miracles are a manifestation of light—love[380]. There are no big or small miracles, as all are expressions of love.

Miracles are natural, and everyone has the right to create miracles. Everyone has the right to love and to be loved, and miracles bring more love to the giver than the receiver.

- **Miracle are thoughts manifested**

Miracles are thoughts in physical manifestation and bear witness to the truth. Miracles rearrange perception and place all dimensions in one true perspective. They enable us to heal the sick, raise the dead, and to dissolve poverty, for we are the creators of these dire circumstances.

Miracles are healing because they supply what we lack. They present freedom from fear and darkness and inspire gratitude. Light and love are the mechanisms of miracles, that is the expression of an inner awareness of the Christ consciousness and the acceptance of 'oneness'[381].

Who can create miracles?

Everyone can create miracles, as everyone has a need, desire, and innate ability to give and receive love. The miracle makes no distinction between degrees of misperception, ignorance, and darkness. It is a device for 'perception correction', that is the birth-right of all.

A major contribution of miracles is to release us from a false sense of isolation, deprivation, and lack. The miracle compares what we have made with our true blueprint of creation, accepting what is in accord with the truth. It rejects what is out of accord, or in discord, and therefore false in our lives.

Miracles are temporary communication devices, and therefore should become habits, occur involuntarily, and should not be under conscious control.

- **Prayer and meditation**

Prayer and meditation are mediums for miracles. Through meditation and prayer, love is received, and through miracles, love is expressed.

Miracles are everyone's right. However, purification, the release of fear, letting go of negativity by being forgiving, are necessary. All miracles mean life, and God is the giver of life.

- **Universal blessings**

Miracles are universal blessings through us, to all of humanity. They are a correction of false thinking and restore our minds to oneness, wholeness, and holiness. By releasing our minds from the imprisonment of our illusions, our sanity is restored.

We become free. Truth, the Universal or Christ consciousness, sets us free. Miracles honour us and honour the divine. The reason, we are all worthy of love, and we are all loveable[382].

Important questions then follow:

- Can we consciously create miracles?
- or at least can we contribute to miracles occurring in our lives?
- If so, how?

Creating miracles in our lives

Yes, we can consciously co-create miracles with Source. This is part of our birth-right. This is part of who we are. We have a DNA success blueprint that holds the key to creating miracles,

However, we first need to understand the spiritual laws that govern these processes, and then make use of these wisdoms in our everyday lives.

In essence, this is very easy. All we need to do is to follow these universal spiritual laws as it paves the way to ultimate success.

The spiritual laws of success and creating miracles

Contrary to all other contributions concerning various spiritual laws—there is only 'one law' for success.

- **The One Law**

This is the law of love—the constant flow of cosmic light—the 'I am presence'—God-consciousness. All other 'spiritual laws' are part of this one universal law. Religion and science have merely approached this from different angles.

It still remains 'one', the 'all-in-all', law. It is the foundation and power that unites all religions, and all dogmatic, academic, scientific, and spiritual approaches. It is 'all-that-is'. Separation and division are only caused by dissociating yourself from the 'one law' or - the Lord[383].

This one law is the 'Love Law'. All you need is found on the level and wavelength of love and compassion. If you need something, then find and give more love. First, start with connecting to and falling in love with the Universe. Then fall in love with yourself – your real-me authentic self. The rest will follow naturally…

- **Miracles - a natural way of everyday living**

Miracles become natural everyday occurrences, once we have learnt to synchronise with universal laws. Einstein gave us direction in his formula $E = mc^2$. It is our task to make a study of these principles, utilise the infinite potential at our disposal, and then use this power to the benefit of all[384].

When you refer back to previous books in this series, book, you will find that we have already covered all the spiritual laws without mentioning them by name. Here follows a short summary of some of these spiritual laws we will abide by in the next season of human existence.

Summary of spiritual laws

- ### The Law of Infinite Potential

We live in a multidimensional universe of infinite energy that can be transformed into infinite possibilities. This law is based on the fact that the true essence of who we are, is pure consciousness. Pure consciousness, pure potentiality, is seeking to express itself into form. This is not only a scientific fact but also a spiritual truth and law.

When we realize that our inner being—the spirit that animates our minds and bodies—is one of pure potentiality, we are then in alignment with the power that manifests everything in the universe. Anything is possible, and there is unlimited creativity. In the process of connecting with and using the infinite power, wisdom, love, and joy of pure consciousness, we discover our true self, the higher self of our essential nature.

The only limits are the ones we impose through our fears, doubts, uncertainty, lack of faith, lack of confidence, or any other lower-level emotion. When you are in alignment with pure potentiality, there is no fear. You are then truly free.

If you know and develop a relationship with Source, and then act 'as if' you were part of Source, you will be in touch with pure potentiality. That is why the practice of meditation is so powerful. When we commune with nature and witness the intelligence within every living thing, we are connecting to pure potentiality.

- ### The Law of Oneness (the Law of Unity/Universe)

There is no separation on a spiritual level. Everything is

connected to everything else. This means 'all-is-one'. At this level, we are connected to everything we desire, want, or need. Lack, poverty, and illness, don't exist here.

They are but figments of our imagination and are wrong or illusionary thinking that needs to be corrected. Oneness includes the Law of Non-Judgement. When you judge another, you judge the self.

Once we live according to this law, the door to health, healing, love, and abundance opens, and all we want, and desire flows into our life.

- **The Law of Right use of Power or energy/life force**

The universe is always in constant flow—nothing is ever stationary. Giving and receiving are different aspects of the flow of energy-information. Affluence, a term used to imply material wealth and abundance, refers to the universality of flow.

Einstein gave us the formula for flow in $E = mc^2$.

It is up to us to use it and to co-create by aligning with this physical and spiritual law. By consciously constructively using our life force and maintaining flow, we keep the abundance of the universe circulating in our lives.

When we are conscious of flow, we are also aware of effortless ease. With this realisation, we become aware of freedom and the ability to co-create miracles.

Become aware of perfection—perfect union in everything – and use it with respect and reverence. Remember, we too are part of this perfection so don't concentrate on your mistakes, failures, and imperfections. Let go and live your 'right use of power'.

- **The Law of Effortless Ease (Flow and Freedom)**

Nature functions with effortless ease, with carefree harmony, and love. Trees are busy being trees, flowers are flowering, bees are being bees, and human beings should be being who they are—spiritual beings.

However, most people have lost the ability to 'just be'.

We can create success and good fortune with effortless ease, when we let go of struggle, resistance or judgment, and harness the universal forces in harmony, joy, and love[385]. We just need 'to be'. If you can accept and not just tolerate circumstances, differences, and similarities, then you will understand the Law of Effortless Ease. This includes the Law of Detachment.

- **The Law of Detachment**

> *"Let go of what wants to be free—*
> *If it comes back it is meant to be"*

The Law of Detachment says, "in order to acquire anything in the physical universe, you have to relinquish your attachment to it."

Detachment is the ability to let go of all personal identification with, and control over, external possessions and positions. Personal investment is relinquished, to evolve to higher levels of attainment[386].

Accepting circumstances as they are, is the first step in changing any unwanted experience. However, acceptance is not condolence—you only accept 'it is so'. Faith in the Universal Law of Abundance can bring good out of any situation—if you allow it to. This is also so with the Law of Allowing. It is all about trust. When we are in a state of detachment, we trust. To be detached from the outcome of a result means that you have learned to trust.

In her book, *The 7 universal laws,* Christy Whitman says that when you know that Spirit will give you what you need—not necessarily what you want (that's ego's job)—then you will learn to do the work that needs to be done and then move on.

The results will take care of themselves. The timing of how things manifest will come at the perfect time. When we trust that the universe knows what perfect timing is, it then happens even faster, because we get out of the way.

If you stand in the way of the energy creating the outcome, or result—through your lack of trust, insecurity, and fearfulness—you put a barrier in the way of the efficiency of that flow of energy (resistance).

By learning to trust, you live in the wisdom of insecurity and uncertainty, where there are unlimited opportunities in the present moment of now. Do you remember the Law of Pure Potentiality?

- **The Law of Non-Judgement**

Judgement is a lower-level emotion. If you are out of alignment with the Law of Allowing, you believe that another person needs to think, feel, believe, and act according to how you think they 'should'. I call this having 'perfect pictures', and this can cause great suffering in your life and your relationships.

This is the opposite of accepting another as they are. If you have a deep-rooted fear that unless everyone thinks, feels, believes, and acts in a certain way— 'your way'—then they are somehow 'wrong', and then you judge them.

'One Law' demonstrates the paradoxes of life.

When you judge, you place the one above, as opposing the other. We need to see the paradoxes in life, as everything has a 'flipside' of the same coin.

- **The Law of Order and Chaos**

The core of creation is silent and still. There is no fuss, no bother, no conflict, and separation. To co-create, we need to consciously connect with our inner core, become still and silent, and then let go of all struggle, conflict, and inner noise.

We all need to enter the holy of holies—the kingdom of God[387]. Meditation, prayer, and silence are tools that we can use to access this level of attainment. Implicit order always includes chaos.

The Chaos Theory has taught us that nothing in physicality lasts forever. Structures and forms integrate to once again disintegrate, to form new structures and forms. Chaos and order are the flipsides of the same coin of reality.

Within this paradox, we find the implicit order of the

universe. Once we understand this law, we do not become perturbed by any external chaos or order. We live from within the silent chamber of the soul, from within—to without.

- **The Law of Resonance (Attracting or repelling forces)**

Everything is resonating as part of the 'one song'—the universe. It is a physical and spiritual law that everything on the same frequency, attracts like.

Everything that is not on a specific frequency is rejected, repelled, or resisted. The Law of Attraction states that whatever is broadcast out into the universe is joined by, or attracted to, energies that are of an equal frequency, resonance, or vibration.

The paradox is that everything that we reject, struggle with, resist, or oppose, becomes a powerful attraction force that attracts to us, exactly what we *don't* want.

In essence, we project our inner struggles on the outside world and struggle with ourselves, in different external forms. The law active here is the Law of Resonance or the Law of Attraction, because 'what we focus on—grows'.

The resonance can be changed by healing inner struggles and letting go of pain, hurt, disappointment, and negativity. You will then attract something new. Because of this law, it is more powerful to stand for something positive—than against anything negative.

There are many ways to express the Law of Attraction:

"Where your attention goes, your energy flows";
"What you focus on grows", "Like attracts like",
"What you think about, comes about"

The Law of Attraction delivers both what is wanted and what is unwanted, depending on the signal we send out to the universe.

You attract what you are, and that which you concentrate upon. If you are feeling negative emotions, you draw in and experience negativity. If you are feeling positive emotions, you draw in and experience positive life experiences. You can attract to you only those qualities you possess.

So, if you want freedom and joy in your life, you must feel what it 'already' feels like to feel freedom and joy in your life—right now! We have been given to challenge to "live as if".

- **The Law of Abundance**

You already have everything within you, right now—to make your life a living dream. Everything is encoded into *potentiality*— 'power on hold'. We just need to release this power into physicality, in whatever form or structure we desire.

We live in universal abundance. The majority have learned to view the universe as one of limitations, and scarcity. There is an unlimited supply of every good and wonderful thing and experience.

There is enough for everyone! We live in an abundant

universe! However, we have bought into the lie that there is not enough, and we must struggle and fight for what we want and need.

This is the lie of scarcity and limitation[388].

Beliefs based on lack affect our ability to manifest our heart's desires. We should come from a space of ease and effortlessness. This lack-mentality controls us, by keeping us longing for what others have, or fighting to be better than others. Most of us feel that who we are, what we have, and what we are doing, is not enough. That is a big lie. You learned about the Law of Attraction. If you feel that you never have enough, that is what you will be attracting into your life. If you feel you are not enough, you are right. If you feel what you have is not enough, you will continue to receive not enough.

Manifestation happens when we can be in a place of feeling at peace with where we are while being excited about the possibilities ahead. That is why it's so important to learn about all the laws, not just the Law of Attraction[389].

- **The Law of Intention (Deliberate Creation)**

Intention or 'in-tension', says it all. We are in a state of tension. We have desires, needs, and wants, and expect them to be met. The tension between where we are, and what we have, with where we would like to be and have—causes tension.

This ignites a process.

If your intentions come from fear of lack, pain, or disease, then this ignites the same process and you get more of what you don't want. However, if your intentions stand the 'fire test', you co-create more of what you do want—as physical manifestations of love-wisdom-power.

When we desire something to manifest from the universe, and we are feeling negative emotions, we are blocking that creation from coming into manifestation.

It is our negative emotions that hold us apart from it. When we release our resistance, we are back in the state of allowing, and all the abundance, freedom, joy, success, prosperity, wealth, and happiness (you name it) can flow to us.

This is also the Law of 'Deliberate Creation' or 'Co-creation'. The Law of Intention is offering a vibration knowingly, consciously, mindfully, deliberately—so that you don't create by default. Most of the time, unless you are aware of these laws, you are offering a vibration unknowingly.

You unconsciously live on a lower level of awareness.

When you don't apply the Law of Intention, you function mindlessly, you are unaware, and you are an observer. You focus on your current reality and you have a vibration (either positive or negative).

The Law of Attraction then responds to that vibration, and you receive more of the same. So, the Law of Attraction can work for you and against you.

It is imperative that we fully understand the Law of Intention, and then we can be aware of how all of these laws work together and affect each other.

This is the One Law in action in various ways.

- **The Law of Paradox and Polarity**

In the paradox of the universe, there are two poles or opposites of everything. Paradox represents the two extremes of one 'thing', which is in fact, the same thing. There is always a flipside to the coin.

One has rich/poor; good/bad; abundance/lack; health/disease—all depending on our perception. By choosing to change our perception and our resulting attitude, we can shift our perception of someone or something, from let's say, 'bad' to 'good'.

This becomes our new reality.

By seeking a higher frequency vibration of energy in this transformation process, the previous lower frequency of vibration of energy gets replaced. 'Bad' can become 'good', for example. The choice made, and the decision implemented, automatically involves the Law of Cause and Effect—reaping what you sow—depending on the choice you made in your responses.

You can raise your vibrations and positively change others. This includes the Law of Cause and Effect. 'What you sow—so you shall reap'. Everything—even our common law, needs to answer to the '*one law*'—the Lord, to be successful and to create miracles.

Law, principles, and guidelines

Some would ask what the difference is between a law and a principle.

- **A law**

Law is a given. Keeping the law has benefits. In this case, the opportunity to co-create miracles with the Universe. The universe is ultimate consciousness and is impatiently waiting for you to 'follow the rules'. The laws have been given to us as a 'short cut' to co-creating your best life ever.

It's like being gifted a fool-proof recipe for success. Everything is in flow. You can create everyday miracles with effortless ease.

Transgressing, ignoring, or violating spiritual laws has consequences. You struggle. Fear, anger, resistance, worry, and negativity are part of your everyday life. It will continue until you clean up and clean out your body, heart, mind, soul, and spirit – hit the reset button – and start again. This time by learning about and abiding by the laws.

Spiritual laws are not there to make life difficult and/or to punish us. These are love-laws. They are universal laws that govern everything and everyone and bind us into one fully functional whole. Although we are unique - we are part of the Universe – the 'One Song'. Laws are meant to keep us in tune with the rest of the Universe that is also the storeroom of everything you want need and desire.

Why make life difficult for yourself by ignoring these spiritual laws.

- **Principles**

Principles are your personal guidelines for your life. You choose to be honest and live with integrity -or not. The ultimate goal of quality living is to align your principles with spiritual law.

- **Guidelines**

Guidelines are given as short-cuts to access what we want and need. For example,[2]:

>Ask – and you shall be given

>Seek – and you shall find

>Knock – and the doors will open

The big challenge is to know exactly what you need and learn how to ask for it. We will cover this in one of the next books in this series.

Please see all references in the original script.[3]

QUESTIONS

Ask yourself:

- How are you currently implementing these spiritual laws in your life? What are the results?
- What has your religion and culture taught you about these laws?
- Do you agree? What has stayed the same? What has changed?
- What do you still need to learn/implement into your life?
- What miracles have you become aware of?
- Have you ever created miracles in your life? How?
- Do you teach others to co-create miracles in their lives? Why/why not?
- What are your heart's desires?

- What is your greatest challenge at the moment? What do you think is the solution? What kind of miracle will solve your problem? Remember – there are no big or small miracles. Ask yourself, "What is the best case scenario? Make it happen.
- What is your next step? Why?

Below you find a few exercises to help you to activate these laws in your life.

EXERCISES

You can implement the following to activate these laws in your life:

Exercise 1: Sit and watch a sunset or listen to the waves of the ocean crash up against the shore or smell the beautiful scent of a flower. Identify how it feels. Become aware that Pure Potentiality created all these things and so much more.

Consciously focus on experiencing your true *self* as unlimited, knowing only love and understanding, and that there is no need to fear. Anything is possible because nothing is impossible. When you are in alignment with the Law of Infinite Potential, you feel centred, at peace, and one with the universe.

Exercise 2: Learn to look beneath the surface of events, possessions, people, and their behaviours. Look beyond academic, religious, business, and political structures, and the people creating these systems. Know they are all just temporary structures and will disintegrate to make place for new thought-forms and structures, that will also integrate and disintegrate.

Knowing this, don't judge. To pass judgement means that you think you know everything—and we don't. Experience a deeper connection to all. Become the silent observer. The only lasting experience is the experience of oneness. See how long you can stay aware of oneness, before your mind drifts off once again, and becomes cluttered and noisy. Practice this every day.

Exercise 3: Think of a time in your life when you experienced everything occurring without struggle—a peak performance, a time you felt on top of the world, a time everything seemed perfect. Identify what you were thinking, what your beliefs were, and how your body reacted.

Become aware of how it felt, what your body was telling you, and how it made you feel. Recreate this experience in your mind. Constantly remind yourself how you feel when in flow. Remind yourself this is your natural state, and do not settle for anything less. Learn to master yourself and the world around you, and then remain in constant flow.

Exercise 4: There are two ways to apply the Law of Detachment. The first is to allow others to be as they are, and secondly, it is to allow (receive) from the universe all that we desire. The keyword here is 'faith'.

NOTES

WHO IS THE AUTHOR - DR BRENDA HATTINGH?

Dr. Brenda Hattingh is an international inspirational speaker, leadership coach and mentor, and business, corporate, and leadership consultant. Brenda invests her time in using personal and organisational power and success potential encoded as our unique DNA blueprint. This is a global first in personal and organisational training and development.

Brenda is committed to the development of a new level of consciousness with an awareness of the value of authentic living and leading. She focuses on assisting people, teams, companies, and organisations – who are willing to bring their *best selves* to the table.

As an author, Brenda brings to the table cutting edge information, books, and training courses that include topics *like Power Intelligence – the intelligence of the future, New Success DNA*, and *New Leadership DNA*. She is Director of the *Power Intelligence Academy* and *The Academy for Authentic Leaders*. Brenda is also the *CEO of the Centre for Power Intelligence*

As an innovator, Brenda is committed to the development of a new generation of successful, innovative, inspired, thinkers, and leaders. She speaks at events and conferences, presents workshops nationally and internationally, lectures at various universities, and has published various books.

Her work is featured on TEDx Talks as Brenda introduces the next season of personal development and leadership training that includes tapping into your DNA-blueprint. Brenda is also the recipient of various awards including the *Professional Businesswoman of the Year Award*.

ENROLL FOR A PERSONAL 5-WEEK COACHING COURSE.

LEARNING TO COACH YOURSELF TO ULTIMATE SUCCESS

This will be one of the best investments you have ever made.

Background

Times have changed and we need to think on our feet. You can only be super successful and flourish if you know how to coach yourself and manage your inner dialogue. Very few people, especially leaders, know how to do this.

At the moment, we are also experiencing a genetic migration. Humanity is going through a transformation, right down to a DNA level. This means we also need to learn how to activate our DNA success-blueprint. The information on how to do this is now available.

Contact us if you would first like to book a free session

What will you learn?

In this beginner course of *Learning to Coach Yourself*, that runs over five weeks, you will learn:

- Who your real-me is and what your personal purpose is
- How to tap into and activate your DNA success-blueprint
- How to master your inner dynamics and create affluence
- How to create the next level of success and happiness
- How to overcome inner blockages and pitfalls
- To understand the psychology of money and affluence
- To understand the science and psychology of real success
- How to become an authentic leader and influencer
- How to create health, wealth, and happiness that benefits everyone
- And much more…

What will you receive:

- E-book 1. Coaching yourself to ultimate success. Who coaches who?
- E-book 2: Authentic living and leading. What is it and how to develop it
- Your personal workbook for your notes
- Five one-on-one personal coaching sessions via Skype, Zoom, or WhatsApp with Dr. Brenda Hattingh.
- Three DNA-healing sessions
- A plan of action/map for the next season of your life.

Books available on www.amazon.com/books

Who should invest in this course?

Everyone who wants to move forward and create their best life. This includes people like you and me, leaders, teachers, parents, business-persons, couples ...

How to book your *Course. Learning to coach yourself?*

Send an email to: info@powerintelligence.net. We will send all the necessary information to your inbox. See our website: http://www.brendahattingh.com

BOOK DR BRENDA HATTINGH AS SPEAKER

To book Dr. Brenda Hattingh as an exciting, entertaining, and inspirational speaker for your next event, or conference and training session, contact us by sending an email to:

Email: info@powerintelligence.net

See website: http://www.brendahattingh.com

oooOooo

BOOK DR BRENDA FOR LEADERSHIP TRAINING

Email us: info@powerintelligence.net

oooOooo

THE POWER INTELLIGENCE LEADERSHIP ACADEMY

See the courses currently available at the Power Intelligence Leadership academy

Website: https://power-intelligence-leadership-academy.teachable.com

MORE BOOKS IN THIS SERIES

Available from. Amazon.com/books

CURING CORRUPTION

Corruption is one of the worst pandemics of our time. Corruption is in essence a mental-health issue and should be treated as such. Unfortunately, current strategies are failing because they don't address the fundamental root cause of corruption.

In the two books below, you will find all the necessary information for you to take in your place as part of the solution to the corruption pandemic.

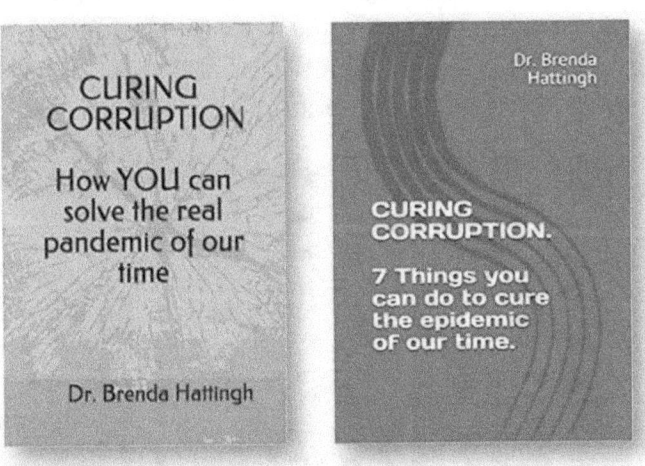

Books available: www.amazon.com/books

ooo0ooo

AUTHENTIC LEADERS IN ACTION

The world is in chaos and dire need of real, authentic leaders. People are awaking and are not afraid to stand up, take in their place, bring peace, build bridges, create a new vision of the future, and shine in their own unique way. These are our authentic leaders.

Such a man was Nelson Mandela.

We accelerate our own awakening, growth, and development by learning from those who went before us.

A course, *Ten lessons from Nelson Mandela...*, is available from https://power-intelligence-leadership-academy.teachable.com. Below you find two books with life-lessons from this iconic leader

 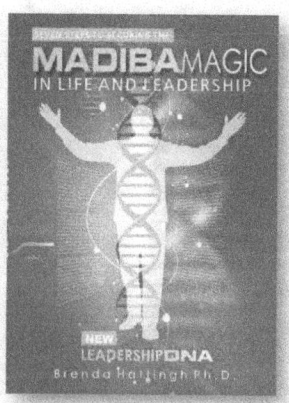

. Available from. Amazon.com/books

REFERENCES

Hattingh, Brenda. (2012 a) *New Success DNA. What is it and how to develop it.* Currency Communications: Johannesburg. Chapter 18

[1] See the list of books in the series: Authentic Living and Leading
- Book 1: The authentic self. Who am I?
- Book 2: Coaching yourself to ultimate success
- Book 3: Authentic leadership. Recovering your DNA leadership-blueprint
- Book available on www.amazon.com/author/brendahattingh

[2] The Holy Bible: St Matthew 7: 7-8

[3] Please see all the other references in the original script:
Hattingh, Brenda. (2012 a) *New Success DNA. What is it and how to develop it.* Currency Communications: Johannesburg. Chapter 18

oooOooo

www.ingramcontent.com/pod-product-compliance
Lightning Source LLC
Chambersburg PA
CBHW070839220526
45466CB00002B/830